JEWISHNESS AND JESUS

Daniel C. Juster

ISBN: 978-1-951833-73-2

Published by:
Lederer Books
An imprint of Messianic Jewish Publishers
6120 Day Long Lane
Clarksville, MD 21029

Distributed by:
Messianic Jewish Publishers & Resources
Order line: (800) 410-7367
lederer@messianicjewish.net

In honor of
Rabbi Manny Brotman,
a pioneer of the Messianic Jewish
movement from the 1960s.

CONTENTS

JEWISHNESS AND JESUS

What is the relationship between Jesus and Jewishness? Several answers are given. Everyone has some idea how the two relate.

An orthodox friend, for example, thinks that Jesus was certainly a deceiver of the Jewish people and responsible for much of the suffering among us. Dr. Samuel Sandmel, professor at Hebrew Union College, states, however, that "Jesus by the standards of first-century Judaism was in all probability a good and loyal Jew."[1] Others say: he was a good rabbi; he was a prophet; he was a misguided leader of a Jewish rebellion against Rome; he was a sectarian ascetic, perhaps a member of the Essenes.

This is an amazing catalogue of responses. But despite the divergence of opinion, to many people one thing seems certain: one who becomes a follower of Jesus is no longer a Jew and forfeits any claim to Jewish identity. Once, in conversation with a rabbi friend, the subject of Jewish identity and various world views came up. I asked,

> "Might a Jew be an atheist and still be considered a loyal Jew?"
>
> "Yes," he said without hesitation.
>
> "A Marxist perhaps?"
>
> "Yes."
>
> "What of a Jew who becomes a Hindu or a Buddhist?" This time the answer was again affirmative, but hesitant.
>
> "Then is it conceivable that a follower of Jesus might yet be a loyal Jew?"
>
> "No, this is impossible." The last response came with conviction.

Yet the facts of history are clear. Jesus himself was a Jew. His original name was *Yeshua*. Jesus derives from the Greek language and is simply an anglicized version of *Yeshua*. In keeping with the sense of the original context of Jesus' life and teaching, I will refer to him as *Yeshua*.

Not only was Yeshua a Jew, but so were all of his first followers.[2] The whole movement for the first several years of its existence was a movement within Judaism. A librarian at a well-known Jewish college told me that the Jewish movements during the first century were once of great interest to him. "It blew my mind," he said, "to find out that all of the early followers of Jesus were orthodox practicing Jews."

Yet we are told that if one is a follower of Yeshua, any claim to Jewish identity is lost. Our original question concerning the relationship between Jesus and Jewishness has led us to a great paradox: How can it be that one who follows a Jew (all of whose original followers were Jews) is no longer Jewish?

Can we unravel the mystery of Jesus and Jewishness? I believe we can if we examine the documents of the history of the first few centuries of the common era.

THE FIRST FOLLOWERS OF YESHUA

The original followers of Yeshua believed that through the life and teaching of Yeshua, they found the clearest exposition of life with God (Luke 24:32; Acts 2:32; Matthew 5-7). They perceived a deeper purpose for their lives, forgiveness and even the certainty of everlasting life with God.

The decades during which this movement first prospered were filled with turmoil. The mighty Roman empire ruled over the nation of Israel. In the most difficult times our people often looked for the coming of the Messiah, the descendant of King David. At his coming we were to be delivered from all oppression. The world kingdom of peace would prevail. It is not surprising then that under the heavy hand of Rome messianic hopes and speculations were nurtured in many sectors of the population,[3] and political messiahs sought to overthrow the yoke of Rome.[4] The followers of Yeshua believed that they had found the one who would eventually return and set up the long-awaited messianic kingdom.

Meanwhile, they occupied themselves with the task of spreading the life-giving message of their master among the people of Israel. They were busy encouraging a spiritual renewal in the Jewish community. Our people have known other renewal movements in their history, but none were like this one. There are some important parallels, however.

For example, the Hasidic renewal movement, like the early movement for Yeshua, caused much opposition among the established leadership, but gained great support among the common people. The Baal Shem Tov also was both praised and maligned. The followers of Yeshua hoped to prepare the way for Messiah's reign by their preaching and new way of living; the Hasidic movement had similar ideas.

The movement for Yeshua provoked much controversy, as did many first-century movements in the Jewish world. Yet no scholar of repute questions the fact that this was a Jewish movement;

the evidence is too strong. Josephus, the first-century Jewish historian, describes James, the leader of the Jerusalem followers, as a loyal orthodox Jew who was greatly respected by his fellow countrymen.[5] A wicked high priest, wishing to eliminate James's disturbing moral presence, had him murdered. However, the righteous moral influence of James was so great that the orthodox Pharisees protested to the governor, and this wicked priest was deposed. Such was the high esteem for James in the Jewish community.[6]

The book of Acts describes the Jewish followers of Yeshua in these terms: "You see, brother, how many thousands there are among the Jews of those who have believed; they are all zealous for the law" (Acts 21:20). We know from other records of history that the communities of Jewish followers of Yeshua after biblical times remained Hebraic, biblical-law-keeping communities in most cases.[7] Jewish heritage and identity were part of following Yeshua.

How is it, then, that Jewish followers of Yeshua are no longer considered Jewish? When did this paradoxical switch occur? Momentous events within Yeshua's movement changed the course of history.

FROM JEWISH MOVEMENT TO GENTILE CHURCH

One of the astounding facts of this early history was that the leaders of the movement for Yeshua became convinced that Gentiles were to be given the opportunity to respond to the message. Extraordinary events created this conviction.

Simon, one of the head disciples, had a vision (Acts 10) that convinced him God's love and salvation were to be offered to Gentiles without requiring them to become Jews in the full, Torah-abiding sense. Rabbi Saul (Paul), a student of Rabbi Gamaliel I, was miraculously touched by God and commissioned to bring the message of Yeshua to Gentiles (Acts 9, 13). This prompted a council of leaders to discuss gentile participation in the movement. After deliberation, the leaders adopted an open-door policy toward Gentiles.

Jews, they decided, are called to a specific task; Gentiles, however, are not necessarily called to be

Jews. Gentiles could be considered accepted by God and one with Jews in faith through Yeshua, if they followed the basic way of life taught by him. (This is parallel to the Jewish notion that the Noahic commands were incumbent upon all peoples.[8] Some rabbis did not believe that righteous Gentiles were called to follow all of the Jewish law but only those Noahic principles.) The council said, in effect, that there could be two wings of the movement of Yeshua — a loyal Jewish wing and a gentile wing. Each group was to consider the other as accepted by God. Neither was to seek to dissolve the other wing into its culture. There could be unity without uniformity; oneness and diversity. Jews were still called to be Jews, but Gentiles were not asked to take upon themselves the whole of Israel's calling as a people.[9]

The issue before the council was the social form of the movement. It is clear from the Scriptures that Yeshua's followers were to reflect the unity of Jews and Gentiles in the Messiah. Table fellowship was the greatest image of this unity. [10] In Jewish areas, the congregations were predominantly Jewish, in gentile areas predominantly Gentile. In areas of mixed population congregations were mixed. All these forms were natural and perfectly valid. There was no quota system for maintaining proportions. This validity remained as long as actions were taken to show unity in the Messiah and acceptance of the others in their various styles of practice and calling.[11]

This decision was a great spur to the movement of Gentiles for Yeshua. Soon gentile followers of Yeshua outnumbered Jewish followers. However, the leadership of living disciples kept the movement in accord with the basic decision of Acts 15. Unfortunately, this understanding was soon lost. The period from 60-90 C.E. has been designated by one scholar as the tunnel period of biblical history.[12] When the dust of war and tragedy settled, the situation had drastically changed.

THE EARLY GENTILE CHURCH

The gentile followers of Yeshua gradually began to understand Yeshua in non-Jewish ways. Though Yeshua and all his first followers were loyal Jews, Jewish practice and identity came to be considered antithetical to what was then dubbed "Christianity." The word Christianity was derived from *Christos*, a Greek translation of the word Messiah. Both mean anointed. The New Testament was written in Greek because it was a universal language. However, this created a gap between the Church and its original Hebraic cradle. The passages in the New Testament condemning hypocrisy among religious leaders were now interpreted as a condemnation of all things Jewish.

The fall of Jerusalem to the armies of Rome (70 C.E.) was taken as further proof to these Gentiles of God's rejection of the Jewish nation and encouraged them to intensify their rejection of the value of Jewish practice and identity.[13] The Church saw itself as the new, true Israel which had replaced the old nation. The claim of the nation was completely dismissed.

Israel as a nation was finished, rejected! This was not biblical theology, for Rabbi Saul (Paul) had declared that the "gifts and the call of God are irrevocable" (Romans 11), and that Israel is "beloved for the sake of their forefathers." This anti-Jewish theology, or what one writer has called the "Christian anti-Jewish polemic,"[14] caused great ambivalence toward the Scriptures, which Christians called the Old Testament. Consequently, Church fathers of the next centuries spoke of Jews and Judaism with great disdain. Though they were men of wisdom, their vision was not free of blind spots. A few tragic examples reflect the direction of the institutional Church.

The epistle of Barnabas at the end of the first century speaks negatively of Jewish biblical practice.[15] H. L. Ellison says concerning this epistle,

> Already the so-called Epistle of Barnabas, which may go back to the last decade of the first century , uses such language about the Jews, Judaism and the Law, as to make

> any effective contact between the two sides virtually impossible. As soon as it had the power the Church did its utmost to defeat God's purpose. It persecuted and bullied, thereby automatically putting itself in the wrong. It spread the vilest calumnies about the Jews.[16]

Ignatius of Antioch in the same century is clear also concerning the uselessness of Jewish things.[17]

Justin Martyr in his "Dialogue with Trypho" speaks in the most condescending terms to his Jewish opponent. Justin could not understand why Jewish followers of Yeshua were maintaining their biblical-cultural identity and practice. They will not go to hell for it, he said, but it is not good. He did not understand that this was their way of expressing their faith in Yeshua and their perceiving his meaning. Justin thought the coming of Yeshua eliminated these things.[18]

Practices developed by the Church were seen as pagan by the Jews. Nothing in the Church persuaded them to see that Yeshua was the Jewish

Messiah, for nothing in the Church appeared to be Jewish. Ellison states that the Church "scandalized them by apparently worshipping images and giving honour to mortal men and women which should have been reserved for God alone."[19] Statutory aids to worship, the veneration of saints and of Mary, summarize how Jews perceived the Church. Loyal Jews could see no sense in being followers of Yeshua.

Even though Judaism was the original context of the faith, the Christian polemic against Jews and Jewish practice continued. With Bishop Ambrose, the theological polemic was translated into external acts.[20] To burn a synagogue was no sin, for the Jews were said to have rejected Yeshua. (This overlooked the great company of Jews who were followers of Yeshua, and in any case, provided no justification for burning synagogues.)

Augustine explained the continued existence of the Jewish community as being only for the purpose of witnessing to the truth of Christianity. The reprobate state of the Jews would prove that the Church alone was true Israel.[21]

The most vitriolic polemic comes from St. John Chrysostom. Chrysostom was upset because many Christians in Antioch frequented the Synagogue seeking to understand their faith through its Jewish roots. This had to be stopped for, according to Chrysostom, Christianity eliminates the value of Jewish practice and identity. To wean Christians from such practices, he painted a picture of the Jews as veritable devils. His eight sermons against the Jews are remarkable for their poisonous hate.

All of this would have been only a manifestation of religious bigotry had it not been for another momentous change: the emperor became a Christian and soon made Christianity the official state religion. The wedding between Church and state translated religious bigotry into economic and social sanctions.[22] The Church-controlled state maintained this posture of discrimination for fifteen centuries.

The images of the "insidious Jew" were the images that prepared the way for Auschwitz. Nazi leaders defended themselves by saying that they were following in this tradition of the institutional

Church. The Church could not understand this because, though it had sought to lower the value of the Jewish people, it had not pursued the implication that the Jews had no right to exist. Since the institutional Church had attributed to the Jew no positive value, there was no Church tradition which could offset Hitler's onslaught.

In fairness we must mention those individual Christians who stood outside of this tradition of death. In their close walk with Yeshua they gained a deep love for Jewish people and risked their lives for their Jewish friends. Sadly, this has always been a small minority of Christians.

Some have stated that the origin of this attitude was the early Jewish persecution of Christians. Although there was fierce persecution against Jewish followers of Yeshua, Jewish persecution of gentile Christians is now considered by the most competent scholars in the field as an unwarranted assumption. There were some minor incidents, but these were nothing in comparison with the hate received.[23]

The irony of all this is that the disciples of Yeshua opened the door to anti-Jewishness by adopting a liberal policy to Gentiles. They were allowed into the movement without being forced to take upon themselves a full Jewish identity. This freedom from cultural restriction spurred the growth of the gentile wing of the movement. Though Judaism was the original identity and way of life in the movement, the gentile majority took over the helm and would not allow Jewish identity within it. During the Inquisition in sixteenth-century Spain, those of Jewish origin who claimed to follow Yeshua were burned at the stake for having Passover seders. The great vision of a Jewish and a gentile wing of one movement, each accepting the other without dissolving the other, was lost.

THE NAZARENES

What happened to the great Jewish wing of the movement? Known to historians as the Nazarenes, Jewish followers of Yeshua broke from the gentile wing and were branded as heretics by the Church because they maintained Jewish loyalty.

Even earlier, the Nazarenes were estranged from the Jewish community. There were several reasons for this. Put simply, however, the majority of the leaders of the Jewish community rejected the Nazarene viewpoint. Through the influence of these leaders, the Jewish community as a whole did not follow Yeshua.

The beginnings of this side of the story are also to be found in the book of Acts. The Nazarene movement reaped the anger from the Jewish community basically for two reasons. First, the community found it difficult to believe that the Messiah could come without setting up the world kingdom of peace. The shameful death Yeshua suffered was incompatible with the common concept of Messiahship. The Nazarene Jews argued that according to Scripture the Messiah would suffer before he reigned as King.

Second, the Nazarene movement stole the gentile proselytes from the Synagogue. There were many gentile pagans, "God-fearers," who saw that Judaism was superior to the pagan religions. Through the work of the Pharisees (predecessors of the rabbis), they attached themselves to the Synagogue. They were not willing, however, to become fully Jewish by undergoing a *mikveh* or ritual bath, circumcision, and taking upon themselves the full yoke of Jewish law. When the Nazarenes offered them the same moral and ethical values they appreciated in Judaism without requiring adoption of the whole of Judaism, Gentiles came in droves to the Nazarene side.

Still, these two sources of tension were not fatal to the relationship between the Nazarenes and the larger Jewish community. There were after all many rival sects within the Jewish community, yet the Nazarenes continued to make headway. The more orthodox in practice among them were not excluded from the Jewish community. Other events proved to be tragically divisive.

The first Jewish revolt against Rome (70 C.E.) was a stunning defeat. Not only were Jewish hopes of independence snuffed out, but reconciliation between Nazarene Jews and the larger community became an unlikely dream. Many Nazarenes did not fight for Israel in this revolt. A minor reason for this was probably that the teaching of Yeshua produced pacifistic tendencies.

The major reason was that Yeshua had predicted the fall of Jerusalem. He counseled his followers to flee for safety when they saw Roman armies approaching (Luke 21:20-22; Matthew 24:15-20). Though the Nazarenes pleaded that they were loyal Jews (and had left Jerusalem in obedience to Yeshua), they were branded as traitors. While some of the people became Nazarene Jews because of the prophecy of Yeshua, the leaders of the Jewish community became hostile. Soon after, a prayer condemning heretics — with Nazarenes primarily in mind — was added to the *Amidah*, the eighteen benedictions which are the standard central prayer of the synagogue service).[24]

Perhaps in time these wounds would have healed. But there was no time. In the 130s C.E. (the Common Era) another revolt against Rome was led by Bar Kochba, this time supported by the Nazarene Jews. They intended to show their loyalty to Israel! They may have thought that this was the final battle leading to the return of Yeshua and his worldwide reign. During the revolt, the venerated rabbi, Akiba, proclaimed Bar Kochba to be the Messiah. The Nazarenes thereupon pulled out of the revolt. Yeshua alone was Messiah. Bar Kochba massacred those who did not give him unquestioned loyalty,[25] The Nazarene Jews were not exceptions. Again, they were branded as traitors despite Akiba's responsibility for his mistake. Jewish tradition retains no honor for the ruthless Bar Kochba, yet the Nazarene Jews were not accepted back into the community.

The Nazarene Jews were thus ostracized by both the Jewish community and the Church. The Synagogue surpassed all rival sects and orthodox rabbinical Judaism became the Jewish view. Church-Synagogue relations deteriorated through the centuries, for both had rejected the only bridge of understanding—the Nazarenes. As the Church and the Synagogue became established in highly defensive postures, neither learned from the other. Nazarene Jews still gained some adherents but, largely ignored, they slowly dwindled until Mohammed destroyed their last communities.[26] The Synagogue rejected the gentile image of Yeshua projected by the Church, and the Church rejected a Jewish view of Yeshua. Through debate and persecution, the theologies of both were honed into sharper opposition.

This tragic story is mitigated by some good. Biblical monotheism, though often in a form unpalatable to Jews, was spread to gentile lands. The Bible was a good and powerful influence in many cultures. The progress of the last two centuries in science can be traced to biblical roots.[27] When the Scriptures became available and were known in the major languages, pagan practice, superstition and magic decreased. Even pagan influences in the Church were greatly eliminated through the Reformation, which stressed knowledge of the Bible.

Between Israel and the Church, misunderstanding still remained. Was there an event at the root of the Church-Synagogue conflict that neither fully comprehended, resulting in tragedy? I believe there was. This event was the life, death and resurrection of Yeshua. A true understanding of Yeshua as a loyal Jew who loved his heritage would be an antidote to anti-Semitism; this understanding is needed by Church and Synagogue. The Church would then appreciate Jewish people, never seeking to assimilate them into the larger gentile community. The Synagogue could find in Yeshua the true son of Israel and the personal embodiment of the meaning of the Torah. A bridge between Church and Synagogue can be made without dissolving the distinctives of either. To clarify these concerns, let's look at last at Yeshua himself.

THE MEANING OF YESHUA

For the nation of Israel, the first century of the common era was a volatile period. Many false messiahs fomented revolt against the hated Roman oppressor, leading time and again to mass crucifixions. Into this turbulent scene came Yeshua.

The records of Yeshua in the New Testament claim his Davidic descent (Matthew 1; Luke 3). He is the one who will be Messiah. Yet it soon becomes quite clear that his purpose at this time of visitation differed from common conceptions of what the Messiah would do. According to prevailing ideas the Messiah would destroy the enemies of Israel and set up a Jewish-dominated kingdom of peace. The very word Messiah inspired revolution. As Yeshua did not come to start a revolution, he was reluctant to use the term Messiah because of these connotations. Thus, Yeshua chose a more neutral phrase, son of man, which he could fill with his own content.

Careful examination of the records reveals several of Yeshua's purposes. One was to teach. As the great rabbi, Yeshua interpreted the Torah in its true, essential meaning. He emphasized the issue of the motives of the heart and not merely the external act. The Torah was the instrument with which he uncovered the underlying motives that led to violations of God's standards.

Speaking on the command against murder, for example, he said,

> You have heard that it was said to the men of old, You shall not kill; and whoever kills shall be liable to judgment." But I say to you that everyone who is angry with his brother shall be liable to judgment. (Matthew 5:21)

In relation to oaths he said,

> I say to you, Do not swear at all, either by heaven, for it is the throne of God, or by the earth, for it is his footstool, or by Jerusalem, for it is the city of the great King. And do not swear by your head, for you cannot make one hair white or black. Let what you say be simply "Yes" or "No"; anything more than this comes from evil. (Matthew 5:34-37)

In other words, complete honesty is the standard of God. A true motive of righteousness needs no oath to assure honesty.

Continuing, Yeshua spoke of sexual purity, saying, "You have heard that it was said, 'You shall not commit adultery.' But I say to you that everyone who looks at a woman lustfully has already committed adultery with her in his heart" (Matthew 5:27-28). The problem must first be handled at this level. Concerning revenge he said,

> I say to you, Love your enemies and pray for those who persecute you, so that you may be sons of your Father who is in heaven; for he makes his sun rise on the evil and on the good, and sends rain on the just and on the unjust. For if you love those who love you, what reward have you? Do not even the tax collectors do the same? And if you salute only your brethren, what more are you doing than others? Do not even the Gentiles do the same? You, therefore, must be perfect, as your heavenly Father is perfect. (Matthew 5:44-48)

With the Torah, Yeshua stressed that vengeance is God's business and not our personal right (Deuteronomy 32). He taught, as does the Torah, that if even our enemy's ox has fallen under its load we should help. Yeshua drew out the implications of this teaching and repeated the Torah's call for perfection (Leviticus 17).

All of Yeshua's teaching emphasized a return to God for forgiveness and an urgent plea for a change of heart. He taught and lived the way of love. Only as people act out of a motive of love that is not self-serving is there hope. In compassionate love Yeshua healed the sick, associated with the social outcast, and even died a cruel death with forgiveness on his lips (Luke23:34). This was Yeshua, the supreme teacher.

Yeshua was also the supreme prophet in the great tradition of the Jewish prophets. To the sinner, the troubled and the needy he offered love and forgiveness (John 4; Matthew 8:10-13). To the religious hypocrite he thundered biblical prophetic denunciations. He was concerned to establish a simpler, spiritual Torah-Judaism that would be applicable to all people.

The religious leaders at that time often despised the common people because they could not live up to the rigorous demands of the ritual tradition,[28] Yeshua condemned this attitude and spoke for a simplified spirituality with depth. It would be applicable to farmers, artisans and traders, not just to full-time students,[29] Yeshua spoke with authority and never rejected the validity of the Torah, for he said,

> Think not that I have come to abolish the law and the prophets; I have not come to abolish them but to fulfill them. For truly, I say to you, till heaven and earth pass away, not an iota, not a dot, will pass from the law until all is accomplished. Whoever then relaxes one of the least of these commandments and teaches men so, shall be called least in the kingdom of heaven; but he who does them and teaches them shall be called great in the kingdom of heaven. (Matthew5:17-19)

Yeshua also came to fulfill the meaning of man being created in the image of God. Scripture teaches that, more than any animal, plant or even the whole material creation, human beings, created in God's image, are supposed to reflect the nature and character of the Creator. We are to reflect this image in wise rulership over the earth, in love, and in the active exercise of our moral capacity. But according to the Bible, all people have fallen far short of God's standards of perfection (Psalm 14:1-3; 53:1-3; Romans 3:23); all have turned to selfish ends instead of godly ends; all worship created things — money, success, power and security instead of the Creator. People are fallen, separated from God, alienated. In the words of the prophets, the covenant has been broken and God has become distant, hidden. We do not sense God's reality and purpose in our lives.

In Yeshua, we see the true meaning of the image of God, undiminished and unmarred.

We see in him what all of us are meant to be like. In his love, compassion, justice and mercy, we also see what God is like. This is how he is the son of man and the true image of God. Indeed, he is the meaning of God focused in human form. The prophet Isaiah glimpsed the truth of Messiah's divine nature when he said,

> Unto us a child is born, unto us a Son is given and the government shall be upon his shoulders and his name shall be called Wonderful-Counselor, Mighty God, Everlasting Father, Prince of Peace. Of the increase of his government there will be no end, and upon the throne of David... to establish it... for evermore. (Isaiah 9:5-6)

Yet amazingly, Yeshua said he came to die. He lived out the true meaning of Judaism. He loved and celebrated the feasts — the celebration of Pesach was one of his last acts before his death. And he even used Pesach symbolism to describe the meaning of his death for us:

Yeshua came to die as an atonement sacrifice for our sins. Yeshua's purpose at this time was not the establishment of the long-awaited, worldwide kingdom of peace. Rather, through his atoning death he opened the way for fallen people to turn back to God. Centuries before Yeshua, the prophet Isaiah explained it best:

Messiah is a suffering servant: He was despised and rejected by men; a man of sorrows, and acquainted with grief; and as one from whom men hide their faces, he was despised, and we esteemed him not. (Isaiah53:3)

He is an innocent sufferer: And they made his grave with the wicked and with a rich man in his death, although he had done no violence, and there was no deceit in his mouth. (Isaiah 53:9)

He is a willing sufferer: He was oppressed, and he was afflicted, yet he opened not his mouth; like a lamb that is led to the slaughter, and like a sheep that before its shearers is dumb, so he opened not his mouth. (Isaiah 53:7)

He suffers for the sins of Israel: By oppression and judgment he was taken away; and as for his generation, who considered that he was cut off out of the land of the living, stricken for the transgression of my people? (Isaiah 53:8)

> *He is the sin-bearer and the means of redemption*: But he was wounded for our transgressions, he was bruised for our iniquities; upon him was the chastisement that made us whole, and with his stripes we are healed. All we like sheep have gone astray; we have turned everyone to his own way; and the Lord has laid on him the iniquity of us all.... He poured out his soul to death; and was numbered with the transgressors; yet he bore the sin of many, and made intercession for the transgressors. (Isaiah 53:5-6, 12)

> *His death is followed by resurrection*: When he makes himself an offering for sin, he shall see his offspring, he shall prolong his days; the will of the Lord shall prosper in his hand; he shall see the fruit of the travail of his soul and be satisfied. (Isaiah 53:10-11)

This last passage shows that the one who laid down his life as an atonement for sin is alive again, and sees the fruit of his atonement. He was exalted after dying in the images of biblical sacrifices.[30] His resurrection provides hope.

Beyond the altar of sacrifice in the ancient temple there was a special room called the holy of holies. It symbolized the place of the holy presence of God and was separated from the rest of the temple by a thick curtain. When Yeshua died this curtain was torn in two, demonstrating the new access to God procured by Yeshua's atoning death (Matthew 27:51). In Yeshua the old sacrificial system was fulfilled and became obsolete, for his sacrifice is the meaning foreshadowed by this system. His sacrifice did not do away with the Jewish heritage of feast and festival and its great testimony to God's acts in creation and history. This aspect of our heritage remains. In Yeshua, however, we have a new, direct access to God without a priesthood or temple system.

So, what does this mean to me personally? Well, God respects man's power of choice, and so, in this age all peoples have an opportunity to turn back to God through the Messiah's work. The Law, especially as seen through the teaching of Yeshua, shows us that we have fallen far short of God's perfect standard. Only perfection will be acceptable to God (Leviticus 17; Matthew 5) so that none of us can possibly approach God on the basis of our own good works (mitzvot). God has provided another way of approach called teshuva ("repentance") in the Jewish tradition. Repentance is turning from sin to God. In teshuva we depend upon God's forgiveness alone (Psalm 51).

In the accounts of Yeshua's death at the hands of Rome and through the plotting of corrupt collaborationists in the Jewish state, we see the terrible results of human evil. All of us are implicated in the dilemma of sin which led to the death of God's anointed. We deserve to suffer and die for our own sins. Yeshua was sinless; he did not deserve to die. Yet the good news of the mercy of God is that when we own up to our own sin, turn from it and identify with Yeshua in his death as the atoning sacrifice for our sin, God accepts and forgives us. Through our spiritual union with Yeshua, we receive a new covenant with God, are given new hearts (Jeremiah 31:31-34; Ezekiel 36:25-27) and are considered righteous by God. Yeshua's righteousness is credited to us. This was the clear message of Isaiah.

Why does God accept us through Yeshua's sacrificial death and resurrection? This is something we cannot fully understand but we can offer some suggestions. Yeshua is the revelation of God's great love and forgiveness. He speaks the word of forgiveness in the midst of a torturous death. Yeshua's death also reveals the terrible nature of human sinfulness. As the supreme representative of Israel and the human race, he dies for us as our proxy. And we, in solidarity with our representative head, participate in his death. These factors work together such that God deals justly with sin while offering full forgiveness in Yeshua's name. His death is the fountain of God's love and forgiveness. Thus, peace and fellowship with God are established through repentance and faith in God who offered and raised Yeshua from death.

There is wonderful good news in the teaching of the Scriptures. They teach that if we return to God on this basis, he will become a reality in our lives. His Spirit, the *Ruach hakodesh* will abide with us. Yeshua's resurrection assures us of a new life with God forever — now and beyond death (John 11:25; 1 John 5:11-13; Romans 10:9-10). Our prayers will be living communication with God. As we live according to God's will by the power of his Spirit, our prayers will be wonderfully answered. As we fellowship with the creator God who is love and justice and follow his will revealed in the Scriptures, we will begin to love all people.

Beneath all the conflicts between the Church and the Synagogue we can now glimpse the true meaning of Yeshua. The meaning of Yeshua is good news — a Jewish message for all the world. As Yeshua's earliest followers were Jews, so Jews today continue to be Jews and to live lives of biblically consistent Judaism. Our identity is not lost in any way, but is fulfilled in the deepest sense. We know God! He loves us and has forgiven us! And perhaps, God willing, Jewish followers of Yeshua can be that bridge of understanding between the Church and the Synagogue that will unite them, without destroying either The paradox of Jesus and Jewishness is solved when we see the meaning of Yeshua. It is a paradox born of fear and prejudice which is best laid to rest. If you decide to be a follower of Yeshua, find a fellowship of other followers and grow in the study of the Scriptures.[31] Seek to live from this day forward for God.

MANY HAVE RESPONDED TO THE GOOD NEWS (NEW AFTERWORD)

Jewishness and Jesus has become a classic and a best seller. This is a revised edition.

Since the first edition of *Jewishness and Jesus,* many have heard, understood and embraced the Good News that is in Yeshua. He Is now Messiah and Lord for many Jewish people.

From a few congregations fifty years ago, there is now a movement that encourages Jewish life and identity for those who have faith in Yeshua. It includes over 300 congregations in North America, over one hundred in Israel, scores in Russia scores in Ukraine, congregations in Europe and South America and even now in Australia.

There are even many Messianic Jewish associations. There is the Union of Messianic Jewish Congregations in North and South America, the Messianic Jewish Alliance of America, The International Alliance of Messianic Congregation and synagogues based in America, the Union of Messianic Jewish Congregations of Russia, a Messianic Jewish Union in Ukraine, and a national fellowship of leaders in Israel and more.

There are also amazing statistics on the numbers of Jews who have faith in Yeshua. Jewish attitudes about Yeshua have greatly changed. The Pew Study and the study of the Barna Group both confirm the changes. For example, The Barna Group study in 2017 found that twenty-one percent of Jewish millennials believe Yeshua was "God in human form who lived among people in the first century." Twenty-eight percent "see him as a rabbi or spiritual leader, but not God." In the Pew Study of 2013, thirty-four percent said that belief in Jesus as the Messiah was compatible with being Jewish.

Messianic Jewish congregations in the organizations mentioned above believe that Jews who come to faith in Yeshua are called to continue to identify and live as Jews. They create congregations to foster the goal of commitment to the Messiah Yeshua in the context of continued Jewish life. Messianic Jews also seek to foster Jewish life for Jews who are in Churches. The new organization, *Yahad b'Yeshua*, is effectively doing this.

Gentiles also join Messianic Jewish congregations because they are in agreement with the goals of Messianic Judaism demonstrate that Jews and Gentiles have unity in fellowship in the Messiah. They are drawn to congregations that maintain an ancient Jewish expression of faith.

Messianic Jewish congregations celebrate the Sabbath and all the Jewish feasts. They foster the rights of passage of the Jewish heritage: the circumcision of the Jewish born babies in the congregation, the redemption of the firstborn son, the *Pidyon HaBen, Bar and Bat Mitzvot,* Jewish weddings, and Jewish funerals with a strong emphasis on the resurrection hope. Messianic Jewish congregations vary in their level of commitment to tradition and ancient expression, just as do the various expressions of Jewish traditional synagogues (Orthodox, Conservative, Reform and Reconstructionist).

Messianic Jewish congregational leaders can answer your questions in person. The congregations provide a place of fellowship, teaching and community. We are glad to help you by providing you contact information for congregations in your area.

ENDNOTES

1. From a personal question put to Dr. Sandmel and from his book *We Jews and Jesus* (New York: Oxford University Press, 1973). Still, Sandmel professes great skepticism of any accurate portrait of Jesus
2. A wealth of evidence is available to support this statement; e.g., Acts 21:20 and the summary of evidence from Eusebius and Josephus given in Hugh Schonfield's *The History of Jewish Christianity* (New York, 1933) o.p., especially chapter 3.
3. See fine summary in Floyd V. Filson, A New Testament History (Philadelphia: Westminster, 1964), Pp. 49-557. Oskar Skarsaune, In the Shadow of the Temple, (Downers Grove, Ill: IVP Academic, 2002)
4. An example would be Judas the Galilean whose revolt ended in crucifixion. For a balanced appraisal of the situation see Oscar Cullman, The State in the New Testament (New York: Scribner, 1956), pp. 14ff.
5. Josephus, *Antiquities, XX*, 9:1 (a first-century Jewish history). This reference is universally acknowledged as accurate. Josephus seems to be writing his history to give a favorable impression of his people to Roman circles. Though Josephus is maligned for his desertion of the war effort (he was a Jewish general), his history reflects positive Jewish motivations. There would be no reason to picture James in this light other than the fact that it was the case.

6. Eusebius. *Ecclesiastical History*, II, 23 (an early fourth-century history).
7. Irenaeus, *Adv. Haer*. (Against the heresies), I, 26 (an early second-century work).
8. Genesis 9; see also Schonfield, pp. 28-29 for summary.
9. For example, through the practice of Shabbat (day of rest), Israel testifies to creation. Resting one day in seven (as God did) witnesses to man's need for regular rest and worship: work does not become a tyranny. Passover is not only Israel's national birthday, but, in God's triumph over all other "gods" signifies that he is Lord of all nations. Succot (dwelling in makeshift booths) warns against trusting in material affluence; it recalls the wilderness wanderings when, as Israel had little material wealth, God provided for all their needs. This heritage points to the Messiah and is not destroyed by his coming.
10. This point is well made by John Yoder in *The Politics of Jesus* (Grand Rapids: Eerdmans, 1972). Yoder explains, "The heresy Paul was struggling against was not that Jewish Christians continued to be committed to keeping the law; Paul was quite tolerant of those who held to such a conviction. He went out of his way to share their ritual faithfulness when in Jerusalem. Nor was it their thinking that by keeping the law they would be saved, for the Jewish Christians did not believe that. The basic heresy he exposed was the failure of those . . . to recognize that since the Messiah had come the covenant had been broken open to include the Gentiles." Ritual laws were not to prevent Jews and Gentiles from showing that they

were brothers by eating at a common table. See also Marcus Barth, "Jews and Gentiles: The Social Character of Justification in Paul," *Journal of Ecumenical Studies*, (Spr. 68). David J. Rudolph, *A Jew to the Jews*, Eugene, Oregon, Pickwick, 2016.

11. Paul's great concern for the contribution being collected, largely from Gentiles, for the Jewish believers in Jerusalem reflects this unity (1 Corinthians 16:1-4; 2 Corinthians 9).
12. S. G. F. Brandon, *The Fall of Jerusalem and the Christian Church* (London: S.P.C.K., 1951). See introduction for explanation. Brandon's point is that events of great import were taking place and we have little source material from the period.
13. This is the central, valid point of Brandon's book.
14. Rosemary Ruether, *Faith and Fratricide. The Theological Roots of Anti-Semitism* (New York: Seabury Press, 1974), pp. 117-139. Superb summary of these points with thorough documentation.
15. *Epistle of Barnabas IV* (a late first-century pseudonymous work).
16. H. L. Ellison, *The Mystery of Israel* (Grand Rapids: Eerdmans, 1966), p. 82.
17. Ignatius, *To the Philadelphians, VI*, 1 (an early second-century letter).
18. Justin Martyr, *Dialogue with Trypho*. (Note the general tone of these early second-century dialogues.)
19. Ellison, pp. 82-83.

20. See account in James Parkes, *The Conflict of the Church and the Synagogue* (New York: Atheneum, 1969), pp. 166-167.
21. Augustine, "Tract against the Jews 6(8)." See also the account in Ruether (pp. 163-181) on Augustine and Chrysostom.
22. James Parkes's research in this area is outstanding. He catalogues the history of legislation in the first eight centuries of the common era.
23. Accounts are found in Ellison, pp. 82-84, Parkes, chapter 4; and Ruether, chapter 3, especially 180-181.

24 Schonfield, pp. 40, 46, 60-63, 88ff. Schonfield's history of the break between the Church and the Nazarenes, and the Nazarenes and the larger Jewish community, has not been surpassed. See also Parkes, pp. 106-115.

25 "0n Bar Kochba" see Parkes, p. 93, and Justin Martyr, *First Apology*, chapter 31, 6.

26. An interesting recent discovery is an Arab community that has Jewish symbolism along with the cross represented in their culture. Could they be vestiges of Mohammed's forced conversions? I am indebted to Dr. Louis Goldberg of Moody Bible Institute for this information. Ray Pritz, *Nazarene Jewish Christianity* (Jerusalem: Magnes Press, Hebrew University, 1988).
27. This point is well-known and has been argued by W. F. Albright, Herbert Butterfield and Alfred North Whitehead in many of their works.

28. For example, the tradition concerning the "am ha-aretz" (the people of the land, that is, commoners) is reflected in the Bible in John 7:49 and various Talmudic passages.
29. In this regard, note the greater response of the multitudes than of the religious leaders in the Gospels (Matthew 21:14-16, 46; Luke 20:19).
30. I am indebted to A. Fruchtenbaum, Jewishness and Hebrew Christianity (New York: Beth Sar Shalom, 1974) and E. J. Young, The Suffering Servant in Isaiah 53 (o.p.) for concepts concerning this chapter of Isaiah.
31. For further reading: Basic Christianity by John R. W. Stott (Downers Grove, IL: InterVarsity Press, 1971), Christianity Is Jewish by Edith Schaeffer (Wheaton, IL: Tyndale Publishers, 1975) and The Lord from Heaven by Leon Morris (Downers Grove, IL: InterVarsity Press, 1974).

ABOUT THE AUTHOR

Daniel Juster, Th.D. Daniel Juster graduated from Wheaton College (Philosophy), and McCormick Seminary M. Div., and Graduate studies in Philosophy of Religion (Trinity University), Jewish Studies at Spertus College of Judaica in Chicago, and a Th. D. form New Covenant International Seminary. He began his pastoral work in the Jewish Vineyard in 1972 and pastured Adat Ha Tikva from 1972-1978, and then Beth Messiah Congregation from 1978-2000. He is the founding President and General Secretary of the UMJC (1979-1988) and is a founder and now senior advisor for Tikkun Global. He was a founding leader of Messianic Jewish Bible Institutes, which now has merged into a program with The King's College and Seminary where he is a professor. He resides mostly in Israel, where he continues to support and mentor Messianic Jewish leaders and communities in the Land. He is the author of many books including *Growing to Maturity* and *Jewish Roots, A Foundation of Biblical Theology*. Daniel is the senior apostolic leader of Tikkun America, a network of Messianic congregations in North America. He leads the teaching and equipping ministry Restoration From Zion along with his wife and Benjamin and Lorena Juster. He has been married to his wife Patty for over fifty years, and they have four children and eleven grandchildren.